Alfaazon Ka Safar

The Journey of Life

SHUBHAM SHELKE

notionpress.com

INDIA • SINGAPORE • MALAYSIA

ISBN
Paperback 979-8-90479-897-0
Hardcase 979-8-90510-380-3

अंतर्वस्तु

About the Author

Shubham Shelke was born to Ratnakar and Sunanda Shelke in Hinganghat, a town in the Wardha district of Maharashtra. He grew up in a close knit family alongside his two brothers and one sister. His family is now settled in Nagpur, a city that stands as a center of growth and opportunity, reflecting the steady progress and aspirations that define his journey.

He completed his Bachelor of Technology in Mechanical Engineering from the Government College of Engineering, Jalgaon, and went on to pursue a Master of Technology in Ocean Technology from the Indian Institute of Technology Madras. He currently works as a Subsea Pipeline Engineer in the oil and gas sector, contributing to complex and demanding engineering projects.

Alongside his academic and professional path, Shubham discovered a passion for writing during his college years. What began as a personal interest gradually evolved into a meaningful way of expressing his thoughts and experiences.

By the nature of his profession and responsibilities, his life is one of constant movement, shifting from one city to another, and often from one country to the next. This continuous journey is not driven by leisure, but by the pursuit of livelihood and the demands of his career. In many ways, he represents the spirit of a modern professional, shaped by discipline, adaptability, and the determination to build a life through hard work across borders.

Deeply grateful to his parents and siblings for their unwavering support and the strong values they instilled in him, he carries those lessons with him wherever he goes. This work reflects not only his growth as a writer but also the resilience, dedication, and perspective shaped by his life experiences.

Preface

Words often carry meanings far beyond what is written, and shayari is one such form where emotions quietly hide between the lines. This book is a collection of shayaris written in Hindi, accompanied by their English meanings so that even non Hindi readers can connect with them. These translations are not exact, word to word conversions, but rather an attempt to express the true feeling and intention behind each line. Sometimes, the depth of a shayari lies not in its words but in what it makes one feel.

This collection brings together shayaris reflecting different phases of life like love, pain, anger, loneliness, and moments of motivation. Each piece represents an emotion that many experience at some point in life. Through these verses, the author attempts to capture the journey of human emotions in their raw and honest form.

The book is a result of nearly eight years of writing. Some shayaris are inspired by personal experiences, while others are born out of imagination, yet all of them carry a sense of truth that readers may relate to in their own way. It is believed that everyone, at some stage in life, goes through these emotional phases, which makes this collection not just personal, but universal.

The idea of bringing these writings together into a book was encouraged by the constant support and belief shown by family and friends, who recognized and appreciated the author's writing. Their encouragement played a significant role in shaping this work, and heartfelt gratitude is extended to each one of them.

This book is meant to be read, felt, and interpreted in your own way. Whether you understand Hindi or read it through the English meanings, the essence remains the same to connect with emotions that are real and familiar.

It is hoped that "Alfaazon ka Safar – The Journey of Life" resonates with you. Happy Reading!

Shubham Ratnakar Shelke

srshelke19@gmail.com

1. इक उम्र गुज़ार दी तेरे बग़ैर

इक उम्र गुज़ार दी तेरे बग़ैर इक उम्र अभी भी बाक़ी है
कहकशान करे और ये तनहाई का साल आख़री हो जाए
अब ना तरसाओ हमे के आ जाओ फ़लक से ज़मीन पर
शायद आपके नूर से ये बेकैफ़ दुनिया रंगीन हो जाए
वैसे तो ये राह-ए-सफ़र इतना बुरा भी नहीं पर
ए नाज़नी तुम आओ तो वीरान ज़िंदगी बेहतरीन हो जाए ।

I spent one lifetime without you, and another still remains.
May the stars align, and let this lonely year be the last.
Do not make me wait any longer, come down to earth from the heaven.
Perhaps your light could color this dull world with life again.
The road of this journey is not so terrible on its own,
But if you choose to walk beside me, dear muse, my empty life may finally become beautiful.

2. कोई साथी हो ऐसा

कोई साथी हो ऐसा जो रुह को छु जाये
कोई साथी हो ऐसा जो दिल को भा जाये
बात हमारी होठो पे ही रुक जाये
जब वो देख के हमे अपनी जुल्फे लहराये ।

I long for a companion who could softly touch my soul,
whose presence alone would feel like a quiet blessing.
Someone before whom every word would lose its courage on my lips,
the moment they look at me and let their hair fall free,
as if time itself pauses, jealous of that single, perfect moment.

3. ये बादल, ये सूरज, ये शांत समंदर

ये बादल, ये सूरज, ये शांत समंदर
ये कम था जो बाग को फूलो से सजा रखा है
यहाँ तो ये आलम है के बादल भी समंदर से मिलने के लिए बेकरार है
और वहाँ पता नहीं बेख़बर ज़ालिम ने कहा डेरा डाल रखा है ।

The clouds, the sun, and the calm sea as if that wasn't enough, the garden was dressed with flowers too.
Here, even the clouds seem restless, eager to meet the sea.
And yet, somewhere else, unaware and cruel,
someone has settled comfortably,
not knowing what they ignore.

4. यु तो जानते नही है हम रुबरु आपको

यु तो जानते नही है हम रुबरू आपको
पर दुआ करेंगे मिले सारी जहाँ की खुशीया आपको
चेहरे की खूबसुरती तो समय के साथ ढल जायेगी
जो दिल के खूबसुरती से प्यार करे ऐसा साथी मिले आपको ।

I may not know you in person, yet somewhere quietly,
I carry a prayer for you that life is gentle with you,
and joy never feels distant.
The beauty of the face will soften with time,
but may you find someone who falls for the way your heart feels,
and stays loving you beyond what the eyes can see.

Thoughts
Feelings
Memories
Poems

5. बतलाए हम भी की मांजरा क्या है

बतलाए हम भी की मांजरा क्या है
कोई हमसे पूछे तो सही
इस मुस्कुराहट के पीछे राज क्या है बतलाए हम
कोई हमसे पूछे तो सही
बतलाए हम क्यूं ख्वाब है हर पल उसे पाने का
अरे कोई हमसे पूछे तो सही
शायर कहते है मोहब्बत एक गलती है
तो क्यों ये गलती एक ही इंसान पर दोहराते है बतलाए हम
बस कोई हमसे पूछे तो सही।

I could tell the whole story, what truly happened, if only someone would ask me.
I could reveal the secret this smile is hiding, if only someone would ask me.
I could explain why every moment is spent dreaming of reaching them, if only someone would ask me.
Poet says love is a mistake then tell me why this very mistake is repeated for the same soul again and again?
I would answer if only someone would ask me.

६. भेजा था हमने परिंदा

भेजा था हमने परिंदा जानने हाल-ए-दिल उनका
दिन बीत गये कई फिर भी कूछ पता ना उसका
इक दिन मिला वो गलियारे मे कहने लगा हमसे
ना मेरे दिल का हाल आज यु बेकरार सा होता
भेजते ना तुम मुझे तो तुम्हारा वफादार मै आज भी होता
क्या करू साहाब मै उनकी अदाओ का वो है ही इतनी हसीन
वरना आज मेरा दिल भी उनका दिवाना ना होता ।

I sent a bird to learn the state of her heart, days turned into nights, yet it returned with no reply. Then one evening, I met it in a narrow alley, and it spoke to me in a weary voice. Had you not sent me, my heart would not be this restless today.
I would still have remained faithful to you.
But what choice do I have, my friend, her grace is painfully beautiful.
Otherwise, even my heart would never have surrendered itself to become her devoted captive.

SOME THINGS
are better said
THAN KEPT
inside...

7. वो बात जो दिल मे

वो बात जो दिल मे छुपाये हो कितने दिनो से
कहदो हमे, ना डरो जमानेसे
लोग तो जिंदगी भर बोलते रहेंगे जनाब
अगर बात होठो मे दबाए रखोगे
तो ना नींद तुम्हे आयेगी ना चैन हमे ।

The words you've been hiding in your heart for so long,
say them to me, don't fear the world.
People will keep talking their whole lives anyway.
But if you keep those words trapped on your lips,
you'll find no sleep for yourself,
and no peace for me either.

8. चलो इज़हार करे प्यार का

चलो इज़हार करे प्यार का कुछ नए अंदाज़ में
जब नज़रे मिलाऊ तुमसे तो अपनी पलके झुका लेना
फिर हाथ थामकर मेरा अपनों सा एहसास दिलाना
भर आए अगर आँखे मेरी तो कसकर गले मुझे लगा लेना
क्यों हर बार हम ही बेचारे प्यार में पहला कदम उठाये
चलो इसबार इज़हार प्यार का तुम इस क़दर कर लेना ।

Let's express our love in a new way,
When I meet your eyes, you shyly lower your gaze,
Then hold my hand and make me feel like I belong to you,
If my eyes fill with tears, hold me tightly in your arms to comfort me,
Why is it always me who takes the first step in love every time?
This time, you take that step and express your love this way.

कुछ बाते
कहने से बेहतर
होती हैं,
बस महसूस
करने के लिए ♡
देखा ✓
सोचा ✓
बात करनी थी
भूल गया...♡

९. एक बार तो यू हुआ

एक बार तो यू हुआ हमे किसीसे प्यार हुआ
उन्हें देखा तो बस देखते रह गया
सोचा चलो जाके उनसे बात करते है
उन्हें मुस्कुराते देखा और बात भूल गया ।

Once, it happened that I fell in love with someone.
The moment I saw them, I could do nothing but keep looking.
I thought I would go and start a conversation,
but then I saw them smile and in that moment,
I forgot every word I had planned to say.

10. ना रातों को नींद थी

ना रातों को नींद थी ना दिन में करार था
जो हाल इधर था वही हाल उधर भी था
ना इज़हार हमने किया ना इकरार उसने किया
इश्क़ में गर इंतज़ार ना किया तो फिर क्या किया ।

There was no sleep at night and no peace during the day.
What I felt on my side, the same was true on theirs.
I never spoke my feelings, and they never confessed either.
But tell me if love did not teach us to wait,
then what did we really do in love?

11. ना ये था की वो चाँद सी ख़ूबसूरत थी

ना ये था की वो चाँद सी ख़ूबसूरत थी
ना ये की हर महफ़िल की शान थी
कुछ था तो बस एक साफ़ दिल
सादा सा पेहराव और गर्दन पे तिल ।

It wasn't that she was beautiful like the moon,
nor that she was the pride of every gathering.
All she had was a pure, honest heart,
a simple attire, and a gentle beauty mark resting on her neck.

12. मैं चलु संग तुम्हारे समंदर किनारे

मैं चलु संग तुम्हारे समंदर किनारे
ये तुम्हारा हाथ अपने हाथ में लेकर
पल में ये सारे ग़म छूट जाये पीछे
अपने पैरो के निशान छुट जाते है जिस कदर
ये जो तूफ़ान समेटा हुआ है अंदर बरसो से
वो लहरे बहा ले जाये उसे अपने भीतर
इतना ही तो ख़्वाब है जहाँ हो तुम और मैं इस दुनिया से परे
जिये अपनी छोटी सी दुनिया बनाकर ।

I imagine walking with you along the seashore, holding your hand in mine.
In that single moment, all my sorrows are left behind, just like footprints that disappear in the sand.
The storm I have carried within me for years, I wish the waves would take it away into their depths.
This is my only dream, a place beyond the world, where it is just you and me,
living quietly in a small world of our own.

13. अब तो इश्क़ हो गया है

अब तो इश्क़ हो गया है जी हमे इस शहर से
हमारे लिए कोई मशवरा है तो दीजियेगा
अब प्यार किया है तो बरबादी तय है
अगर हुआ है इश्क में कोई आबाद तो दिखाइयेगा ।

I've fallen in love with this city, slowly, helplessly.
If there is any wisdom you carry, now is the time to offer it.
For once love takes root, ruin is said to follow.
And if love has ever built someone instead of breaking them,
then show me that rare soul
which I have yet to see one.

14. जुल्फे सवारे तो कयामत ढा जाए

जुल्फे सवारे तो कयामत ढा जाए
नैना ऐसे की पूरा समंदर डूब जाए
खुबसूरती ऐसी की चांद भी शरमा जाए
सुनो तुम काला टीका लगाया करो
न जाने कब मेरी ही नजर लग जाए ।

When you fix your hair, it feels like chaos unfolds,
your eyes are so deep, they could drown an entire ocean.
Your beauty is such that even the moon would blush in shame.
Listen, do wear a protective black mark,
who knows when my own gaze might cast an evil eye.

15. तुम्हारा मिलना कोई जादुई सपना तो नहीं

तुम्हारा मिलना कोई जादुई सपना तो नहीं
जो उस खुदा की बनाई हुई नायाब कला हो तुम...
तुम्हे पढ़ना, समझना सब व्यर्थ है
जो सिर्फ महसूस किया जाए वो एहसास हो तुम...
किसिके लिए इंतजार करना मुझे अब गवारा नहीं
सदियों इंतजार करू जिसका वो खास इंसान हो तुम...
प्यार, इश्क, मोहब्बत चाहे जो नाम दो
मेरी सुबह का पहला और रात का आखरी खयाल हो तुम ।

Your meeting me is no magical dream,
you are a rare art shaped by God's own hands.
Trying to read you or understand you is pointless
you are not meant to be understood, you are meant to be felt.
Waiting for someone is no longer something I can bear,
yet for you, I would wait for centuries because you are that special one.
Call it love, desire, or devotion by any name you wish,
you are the first thought of my morning
and the last thought before I fall asleep at night.

16. तेरे किनारे पर बैठ कर

तेरे किनारे पर बैठ कर थोड़ा सुकून मिल गया
जैसे टुटे तारे को फिरसे आसमान मिल गया
हम तो सोच मे पडे थे अपनी उलझनो के साथ
वो आकर इक दफा सुलझाकर चला गया।

Sitting beside you, I found a moment of peace,
as if a fallen star had found its way back to the sky.
I was lost, tangled in my own confusions,
and you came,
untied them, set everything in place,
and walked away quietly.

17. आँखे बंद करु तो सामने आती हो

आँखे बंद करू तो सामने आती हो
फिर अगले ही पल गायब हो जाती हो
आती हो तो कुछ पल रूक जाया करो
क्यू हमसे यु लुकाछुपी खेल रही हो
तुम यही हो क्यूँ मुझे आहट सी हो रही है
ये वहम है या न जाने तुमसे चाहत बढ गई है
सर्द हवा है और फिर खूबसुरत सी शाम
कर दो ना शाम आज हमारे नाम ।

When I close my eyes, you appear before me,
and the very next moment, you vanish again.
If you come, stay for a while.
why do you keep playing hide and seek with my heart?
You're right here... why does this feeling feel so real?
Is it just an illusion,
or has my longing for you quietly grown deeper?
The wind is cold, the evening draped in quiet beauty
will you let this evening belong to me?

18. अगर रूठ जाऊ कभी तुमसे

अगर रूठ जाऊ कभी तुमसे दिल-ए-नादान
तो पास आकर तुम मना लेना मुझे
बेहद प्यार है तुमसे तभी तो गुस्सा करते है
पर यू नाराज होकर तू भी ना अकेला कर मुझे ।

If ever my tender, foolish heart turns away from you,
come closer, don't wait
and softly bring me back to you.
It is only because my love runs so deep
that even my anger is born from affection.
But don't let that moment of hurt
turn into distance between us,
don't leave me standing alone with it.
Stay. Hold my nearness as carefully
as I hold you in my heart.

19. मैं शायरी लिखू और तुम्हारा जिक्र ना हो

मैं शायरी लिखू और तुम्हारा जिक्र ना हो ये मुमकिन नहीं
शायरी की तरह ज़िंदगी में भी होती तो बात कुछ और होती
ये तमन्ना थी की मिले कभी आपसे तो ये दिल भी रूबरू देखे आपको
इन बेज़ार आखों को तुम्हारा दीदार होता तो बात कुछ और होती
समझा लिया है मैंने दिल को ये तुम्हारे ख़्वाब ना देखे
ख़्वाबो में सताती हो, हक़ीक़त में भी सताती तो बात कुछ और होती
यू तो गुज़ार लेंगे हम ये ज़िंदगी का राह-ए-सफ़र अकेले
पर तुम्हारा हाथ मेरे हाथों में होता तो बात कुछ और होती ।

It isn't possible for me to write poetry and not mention you.
If you were part of life the way poetry is, things would feel very different.
I once wished that if I ever met you, my heart could truly see you face to face.
If these tired eyes had been granted even a glimpse of you, things might feel different.
I have made my heart understand not to dream of you anymore. Yet you trouble me in dreams, if you troubled me in reality too, things would feel very different.
I will somehow walk this long road of life alone, but if your hand were in mine, things would feel very different.

Le Café
Today
WE'RE
CLOSED

20. वो कल की ही तो बात है

वो कल की ही तो बात है इतने दूर होकर भी तू पास था
आज तेरे इतने पास होकर भी क़ितने दूर है
तेरे शहर में आकर अब तुझसे मिलने को बेक़रार है
लेकिन ये मेरी कैसी मजबूरी है जिसे मिलने सें इनकार है ।

It feels like only yesterday, though miles apart, you were close to me.
Today, even standing so near, you feel impossibly distant.
I am in your city now, restless to meet you,
yet bound by a strange helplessness
that refuses to let me come and meet you.

21. जिसके नाम से होठों पर खिलती

जिसके नाम से होठों पर खिलती
उस प्यारी सी हसीं का राज हो तुम
जिसे सामने देखते ही चमक उठती
उन बेजार आखों का इंतजार हो तुम
जो मुक्कमल ना हो सकेगा इस जनम में
वो टूटा हुआ अधूरा ख्वाब हो तुम
मैं तो चाहता हु की मैं गलत साबित हूं
पर सच तो ये है की.......
मेरा पहला और आखरी प्यार हो तुम ।

You are the secret behind that sweet smile
that blooms on my lips whenever your name is spoken.
You are the wait within those tired eyes
that begin to shine the moment they see you.
You are that broken, unfinished dream
that will never be whole in this lifetime.
I wish with all my heart that I am proven wrong,but the truth remains
you are my first love,and you are my last.

Some things are never meant to be...
Memories stay. People don't.
Better Days

22. अगर बसर-ए-जिंदगी बस एक बार का तौफा है

अगर बसर-ए-जिंदगी बस एक बार का तौफा है
तो उसे हासिल-ए-जिंदगी सब कुछ क्यों नही?
उसने फूलों से दोस्ती की साथ में काँटे भी आ गए
अगर इतना चुभता है तो वो जताता क्यों नहीं?
उसने तो फ़क़त चाहा था के वो भी चाहे उसको
अगर इतना ही रुलाता है तो उसे भुलाता क्यों नहीं?

If living this life is a gift granted only once,
why doesn't it give us everything we seek from it?
They befriended the flowers,
and the thorns came along as well.
If it pierces the soul like this,
why is it never given a voice?
All they ever wished was to get love in return.
If that love brings only tears,
why don't they just let go and forget?

FOCUS
GROWTH
EXPERIENCES
FUTURE
NEW
CITY
NEW
BEGINNINGS
NEW CHAPTER
NEW YOU

23. ये वक्त किसी के लिए नहीं रुकता

ये वक्त किसी के लिए नहीं रुकता
तो फिर क्यों बीती बातों का शोक मनाया जाए
नया शहर है, नए लोग है
तो क्यों ना फिरसे जिंदगी का लुफ्त उठाया जाए ।

Time does not pause for anyone,
so why should we mourn what has already passed?
It's a new city, with new faces all around
so why not begin again
and let ourselves enjoy life once more?

They left.
They judged.
They thought I'd break.
They were wrong.
FOCUS
DISCIPLINE
GROWTH
FAITH
BUILT NOT BROKEN
SUCCESS
SELF BELIEF
HARD WORK
PATIENCE
SILENCE
STRUGGLE
BETRAYAL
REJECTION
PAIN

24. उन्हें लगा होगा मैं बिखर जाऊंगा

उन्हें लगा होगा मैं बिखर जाऊंगा उनके जाने से
शायद अभी वो वाकिफ नहीं थे मेरे किरदार से
जिसने जब जब मुझे गिराना चाहा है
मैंने तब तब खुदको पहले से ऊपर ही पाया है ।

They must have thought I would fall apart when they walked away,
perhaps they did not yet know my true character.
For every time someone tried to push me down,
I found myself rising higher than before.

For You

25. जिन फूलों को सजाया था राहों में तेरी

जिन फूलों को सजाया था राहों में तेरी
उन्हें तुम बिखेरे चले जा रहे हो
सुनो, हमसे कोई नाता है भी क्या तुम्हारा
या अपने ही धुन में जीये जा रहे हो ।

The flowers I once laid carefully along your path,
you keep scattering as you walk on.
Tell me, do you share any bond with me at all,
or are you simply living on,
lost in the tune of your own world?

Maybe in
your eyes,
I'm not enough..
But in my heart,
you are
everything
Can't hate you.
Can't leave you.
Can't forget you.
Some bonds
can't be
broken
No matter what
It's always you
Memories

26. रुठना चाहु भी तो

रुठना चाहु भी तो मैं तुमसे रुठ नही सकता
सिवाय मोहोब्बत के तुमसे कुछ और मैं कर नही सकता
तुम्हारी नजरो मे चाहे मैं बुरा ही सही
पर दिल से तुम्हे जुदा मैं कर नही सकता।

Even if I wished to turn away from you,
I find I simply cannot.
With you, there is nothing I know
except how to love.
In your eyes, I may be at fault,
yet from my heart,
I can never let you go,
you are stitched too deeply into it.

Still Waiting, Still Hoping...

27. हा तू चाँद है

हा तू चाँद है तेरे चाहने वाले तो कई होंगे
उन चाहनो वालो मे हमारा भी तो नाम है
तुम तो बडी खामोशी से बादलो मे छुप जाते हो
पर जानलो ये सुनापन बडा शोर मचाता है
यु दूरी बनाकर तुम कैसे रह लेते हो हमसे
तुम्हे खो ना दु मुझें तो हरवक्त ये डर लगा रहता है
इक उम्मीद है कल तुम जरूर निकल आओगे
बस कबसे यही इक हम आस लगाये बैठे है।

Yes, you are the moon, and there must be many who adore you.
yet among all those names, mine belongs there too.
You hide so quietly behind the clouds, but know this
your absence makes the silence unbearably loud.
How do you manage to keep this distance from me so easily?
when I live with the constant fear of losing you.
Still, I hold on to one hope that tomorrow, you will emerge again.
And it is with this hope alone that I have been waiting, for so long.

Some things change...
Some feelings don't...
Some people stay...
memories don't fade easily
Time changes... Feelings don't
Some distance... Some Silence... Some stories Never ends...
Memories
Moments
Feelings
Us

28. कुछ चीजे बदल रही है

कुछ चीजे बदल रही है धीरे धीरे
कुछ चीजो पे हक हमारा आज भी है
कोई तरस रहा है पास आने को
तो किसींको दूर रहने मे ही मजा है
कोई बस उन बेजान तस्वीरो मे कैद है अब
तो कोई दिल मे घर बनाये बैठा आज भी है
निकाल लिया करो थोडा वक्त हमारे लिये भी
ना भुलना कभी हमारे दिल मे बसते आप आज भी है ।

Some things are changing, slowly and quietly,
yet some things still belong to me.
Someone longs to come closer,
while someone else finds comfort only in distance.
Someone now exists only within lifeless photographs,
while someone else still builds a home inside the heart.
Take a little time out for me too, once in a while
and never forget,
you still live in my heart, even today.

Some goodbyes never end... They just become memories. ♡
Why her ?
Why not me ?
03:12 AM
Memories
What could've been
If only...
Unsaid words
I wish you were here. ♡

29. क्यूँ यु बार बार मेरे ख्वाबो मे

क्यूँ यु बार बार मेरे ख्वाबो मे आके सताती हो
जाना ही है तो पुरी तरह जाओ ना
तुम तो बडी इतमीनान से आराम फरमा रही होगी
थोडा मुझे भी तो चैन से सोने दो ना ।

Why do you keep invading my dreams, night after night,
just to torment me?
If you've already decided to leave, then leave completely.
You must be sleeping in peace, comfortably untouched,
at least spare me this cruelty
and let me rest as well.

Some eyes speak more than words.
Be careful who you trust
Not everyone deserves your real you
Trust your intuition.
Some conversations stay with you forever.
Some smiles hide more than happiness
Not every smile is innocent.
People change.
Memories don't.
Lessons remain.

30. ऐसे ना देख हमे

ऐसे ना देख हमे इन कातिल नजरो से
पिघलने का दौर अब नहीं
यूं जो तुम बिना बात के मुस्कुरा रहे हो
साजिश लग रही है सादगी नही ।

Don't look at me with those dangerous eyes so softly,
I don't melt the way I once did anymore.
And that smile you wear without a reason
it feels less like innocence
and more like a gentle trick of yours.

31. कुछ सवाल है मेरे दिल में

मेरे अंदर बोहोत घुटन सी हो रही है
कुछ सवाल है दिल में पूछने दोगे क्या?
अगर किसी महफिल में जिक्र हो नाम का तुम्हारे
मन-ही-मन मुस्कुराने की इजाजत दोगे क्या?
मिल जाए अगर किसी अनजान राह पर
नए दोस्तो से पहचान भी कराओगे क्या?
यूं जो तुम बार बार दूर जाने की बात करते हो
अगर हम चले गए तो सच में सह पाओगे क्या?
इस दुनिया से परे दिल में खास जगह थी तुम्हारी
क्या गलती थी हमारी एक बार बताओगे क्या?
कुछ सवाल है मेरे दिल में
दिल पे हाथ रखकर सच बताओगे क्या?

There is a quiet suffocation growing inside me, questions gathering like unspoken prayers in my heart, will you allow me to ask them?

If your name drifts into a gathering somewhere, will you grant me the right
to smile softly, just to myself?

If we cross paths one day on an unfamiliar road, will you introduce me
as someone who once belonged in your story, even to your new friends?

You speak so often of distance, of leaving again and again but if I truly walk away, will your heart really know how to endure it?

Beyond this world, there was a sacred corner of my heart
reserved for you.
Tell me, what was my fault, tell me once, honestly.

These questions rest heavily within me. With your hand
upon your heart,
will you meet my eyes and tell me the truth?

32. क्यू इतनी दूर खडी हो

क्यू इतनी दूर खडी हो
मेरे नजदिक तो आओ जरा
बोहोत धुंधली सी दिखाई दे रही हो
'ऐ किस्मत' क्या यही है वजुद तेरा ।

Why do you stand so far away?
Come closer and let me see you clearly.
From here, you blur into uncertainty.
Tell me, O fate,
is this all you are meant to be?

33. ज़िंदगी की उलझन

ज़िंदगी की उलझन में इस कदर खो गए
कुछ ख़बर ही नहीं है यारों की महफ़िल से
याद तो आती है पर मजबूर है हालात से
तुम पुकार लगाओ तो रुख़ मोड़ लेंगे जमाने से
ये जो धागे मिले थे दोस्ती के आपके आने से
उनकी गाठ ना छुटेगी फिर किसी बहाने से ।

Life's chaos wrapped itself around me so tightly
that even friends laughter faded into distance.
I remember you every day,
yet circumstances stand like chains between us.
Raise your voice just once,
and I will rebel against the world itself.
The bonds of friendship formed by your arrival
are knotted too deep that
no storm, no excuse
can pull them apart.

34. इक दौर था

इक दौर था जब कहानीया भी सच लगती थी
आज तो हकीकत पर भी शक हो रहा है
ना कोई आशिया था तब फिर भी रंगीन थी जिंदगी
आज सबकुछ होकर भी क्यू ये बेरंग सी लग रही है ।

There was a time when even stories felt real,
when faith came easily, without proof.
Now, even truth itself
feels uncertain, fragile, questioned.
Back then, I had no shelter to call my own,
yet life shimmered with color and warmth.
Today, surrounded by all that I once wanted,
I wonder why everything
feels so strangely colorless,
so painfully hollow.

आओ मिलकर
समाज को रोशन करें
शिक्षा है
सबसे बड़ा
उपहार
संस्कार
से ही
सुन्दर है
व्यवहार
नारी का सम्मान
ही सच्ची पूजा

35. अंधेरा बढ रहा है समाज मे

अंधेरा बढ रहा है समाज मे चलो ज्ञान का दिया जलाते है
शिक्षा से वंचित बच्चो के जीवन मे रोशनी लाते है
बिगडे हुए को संस्कार का पाठ पढाते है
लक्ष्मी को पूजने से पहले उनको नारी की ईज्जत करना सिखाते है
चलो इस बार दिवाली हम कुछ अलग तरह मनाते है
क्यू ना हम इसबार भगवान से पहले अपने माँ बाप को पूजते है ।

As darkness spreads deeper through our society,
let us rise and light the lamp of knowledge.
Let us bring hope and brightness
into the lives of children denied education,
and teach values to those who have lost their way.
Before worshipping goddess,
let us first teach respect for women.
This Diwali, let us choose a different path,
not just lighting lamps, but igniting conscience.
Why not, this time, bow our heads first to our parents,
for no god stands higher than those who gave us life.

DREAMS
MEHNAT
SABR
VISHWAS
TANHAI
TOOFAN

36. सपनो के काफ़िले कांधे पे ले चला हूँ

सपनो के काफ़िले कांधे पे ले चला हूँ
मैं हमेशा उम्र से आगे ही चला हूँ
वो क्या जाने तकलीफ़ - ऐ - दास्तान इस दर्द की
जिन्हे मैं सिर्फ हसते हुए मिला हूँ ।

I carry caravans of dreams on my shoulders
and walk a path far ahead of my years.
How could they ever understand
the weight of this untold pain,
those who have only ever seen me smile
and never the battles I wage in silence.

37. कोई चाहे बंगला गाड़ी

कोई चाहे बंगला गाड़ी
चाहे कोई घर परिवार
कोई मांगे दोस्तो का साथ
तो मांगे कोई पिया का हाथ
हमेशा मनचाहा मिलेगा
है ये एक सवाल
पर निराशा पे आशा की किरण
होता है ये नया साल ।

Some dream of a grand house and a fine car,
some wish for a home filled with family.
Some ask for loyal friends by their side,
some seek simply a beloved's hand.
Will life always give us what the heart desires?
That question lingers on.
Yet the New Year arrives
as a ray of hope
shining through disappointment.

शहर
रोजगार

38. ये जवानी भी बड़ी अजीब है

ये जवानी भी बड़ी अजीब है साहाब
घरवालों के लिए घरवालों से ही दूर जाना पड़ता है
जहां यादें बुनी थी बचपन की सारी
उस आंगन को छोड़ शहर कमाने जाना पड़ता है ।

Youth carries a strange kind of truth, my friend
to stand for one's family,
one must first walk away from them.
The courtyard that held every childhood laugh and tear
is left behind,
one must go to the city
to earn a living.

बीज बोया
जन्म दिया, परवरिश की
फ़ल-ओ-फूल दिए
खुशियाँ, संस्कार और
अच्छे मूल्य दिए
आँधियों से बचाया
हर मुश्किल में
साथ दिया
खुद जागे, हमें सुलाया
अपनी नींदें खोकर
सपने हमारे संजोए
माँ-बाप
संवारा, सुधारा
गलतियों पर समझाया,
रास्ता दिखाया
खुद जले धुप में
ताकि हम चल सकें
छाँव में
त्याग
संस्कार
ममता
धैर्य
संघर्ष
प्रार्थनाएँ

39. ये जो फल-ओ-फूल तुमने देखे

ये जो फल-ओ-फूल तुमने
देखे शाख़-ए-दरख़्त पर
कभी जानना की क्या क्या
गुज़री होगी उस शज़र पर
सर्दी, आँधी, तूफ़ान न जाने
कितना कुछ झेला खुदपर
ये जो आज तुम हमे क़ाबिल
बता रहे हो ए दोस्त
वो सबब मोहताज है उनके
जीवनकाल की तपिश पर ।

You see the fruits and flowers growing on the tree branches,
but have you ever wondered what that tree went through?
Cold winters, strong winds, raging storms
it endured so much on its own.
So when you call me capable today, my friend,
remember it is shaped by the struggles and sacrifices my parents lived through.

40. चलते चलते ठोकर लगी

चलते चलते ठोकर लगी तो ध्यान आया,
बीती बातों का फिर मलाल आया
मैं इस भरम में था के कोई दुख दे गया है मुझे
मुद्दतों बाद समझ आया, था वो मेरा ही साया ।

As I was walking along, I stumbled, and in that brief moment something became clear to me.
Old memories stirred, and the familiar ache of the past returned uninvited.
For the longest time, I had believed that someone else had caused me this pain,
that it had been handed to me by another.
But after many years, I finally understood the truth that it was never anyone else at all.
It was only my own shadow walking beside me.

41. क्या तुम्हे भी

पढ़ते पढ़ते हल्की सी कोई याद हमारी
क्या तुम्हे भी सताती है?
कोई मेरे नाम की पुकार लगाये तो
क्या नजर तुम्हारी भी मुझे ढूंढने लगती है?
कोई हमारी थोड़ी सी तारीफ कर दे तो
क्या आँखे तुम्हारी भी भर आती है?
कितनी भी कोशिश करले भुलाने की फिर भी
क्या सपनों में तुम्हे भी मेरी याद बार बार आती है?
मुंह पे चाहे बुराई करलो झगड़ा करलो लेकिन दिल से
क्या फिक्र तुम्हे भी मेरी होती है?

While you're lost in words, does a faint thought of me ever drift into your heart?
When you hear my name somewhere, does your heart pause for a moment, and your gaze look for me?
If someone speaks good of me, does it bring tears to your eyes with the fact that why we are no longer we?
However much you try to forget me, do I still come back night after night, in your dreams?
Even if you argue and speak ill of me openly, does a quiet corner of your heart still care for me?

पता है अब कुछ नही हो सकता बावजूद इसके
क्या बार बार तुम भी मेरी तस्वीर
देखते रहती हो?
अंदर से तो टूट चुकी हो लेकिन
क्या तुम भी खुशी का बस नकाब डालें फिरती हो?
याद हमारी ज्यादा सताने लगे तो
क्या तुम भी अकेले में रो लेती हो?
बात करने का दिल तो बहुत करता है लेकिन
क्या तुम भी खुद को रोक लेती हो?

You know nothing can happen anymore, the ending has already chosen itself. And still, in quiet moments, I wonder do you see my picture now and then?
I know you're already broken somewhere deep within, yet you move through the world carrying a borrowed smile.
Does happiness rest on you like a careful disguise, worn to protect the cracks no one is meant to see?
Tell me, do you still hide your pain behind that mask?
When my memories begin to trouble you too much, do you quietly step aside, let the tears come and go on their own, accepting them in silence, without asking why?
When you feel like talking, when words begin to gather quietly inside you, do you also pause and hold yourself back, choosing silence over voice, the way I do?

42. ऐ जिंदगी सुन

ऐ जिंदगी सुन, कभी मुझसे मिलने आया कर
मुझसे बातें कर, थोड़ा वक्त बिताया कर
इतना तेज़ ना भाग तू भीड़ के साथ
वक्त को थामकर, थोड़ी चैन की साँस लिया कर
तुझसे मिलने के लिये अब मैं
कुदरत से वक्त चुराना चाहता हूँ
सुन, मैं आज फिरसे मैं होना चाहता हूँ ।

O life, listen to me once. Come closer, not in haste, but with patience.
Sit with me for a while, speak softly, or say nothing at all.
Do not run so fast with the noise of the world. Pause.
Hold time still for a moment, let my breath fall into rhythm, let my heart rest.
I have been chasing, carrying, enduring, now I seek only a little peace.
To meet you like this again, I am willing to steal a few moments from nature's silence.
Let me step away from what I became, and return, quietly and honestly, to who I truly am.

43. झूठ का नकाब

इस बनावटी लोगों की दुनिया में रहते रहते
मेरे चेहरे पर भी नकाब सा चढ़ गया है
ख़ुश होना और दिखाना दो अलग बातें है
अब किसीकी याद आये तो खुलकर रोना चाहता हूँ
मेरी प्यारी सी मुस्कान अब लौटा दो मुझे
झूठ का नकाब हटाकर अब सच मे जीना चाहता हूँ
सुन, मैं आज फिरसे मैं होना चाहता हूँ ।

Living so long in a world of rehearsed faces,
a mask has slowly settled over my own.
Feeling happy and showing happiness
have become two very different acts now.
When memories return, I no longer want to hold my tears back,
I want to cry freely, without hiding. Give me back my gentle smile,
the one that once belonged to me. I am tired of wearing borrowed truths.
I want to peel away this mask of lies and finally live honestly, fully.
Listen… today, once again, I just
want to be who I truly am.

44. दोस्तो के साथ गुज़ारे

दोस्तो के साथ गुज़ारे कुछ यादगार लम्हो को
दिल मे ही कैद रखना चाहता हूँ
याद कर उन लम्हों को फिर कभी
मन ही मन मुस्कराना चाहता हूँ
लौटा दो वो दोस्त जो मेरे थे
आदत उनकी मैं बरकरार रखना चाहता हूँ
सुन, मैं आज फिरसे मैं होना चाहता हूँ ।

I want to keep the few unforgettable moments
I spent with my friends safely held within my heart.
And someday, remembering them again,
I want to smile quietly, just to myself.
Give me back the friends who were once mine,
I want to keep their presence alive within me,
the comfort of their habits, the warmth of who we were together.
Listen... today, once again, I just
want to be who I truly am.

45. एक अरसा हो गया चैन से सोए हुए

एक अरसा हो गया चैन से सोए हुए
अब दिल से थकान मिटाना चाहता हूँ
माँ थपकियाँ लगाकर लोरी सुनाओ ना
मैं तेरी गोद मे फिरसे सोना चाहता हूँ
लौटा दो वो हसीन बचपन मेरा
मैं अब हर पल खुश रहना चाहता हूँ
सुन, मैं आज फिरसे मैं होना चाहता हूँ ।

It feels like ages since I last slept peacefully;
now I only wish to let the tiredness drift out of my heart.
Mother, rock me gently, sing to me softly.
I want to fall asleep once again in the safety of your lap.
Return to me those tender days of childhood,
when happiness came without effort or reason.
I want to smile again with that same innocence,
to feel joy as something natural and close.
Listen…in this fragile moment, today once more,
I simply want to be me again.

46. मंजिल किसींको यु ही नही मिलती

मंजिल किसींको यु ही नही मिलती सिर्फ सोचने से
अपने पर कुतर दिये जाते है
बस उडने का ख्वाब देखने पे
जो तुफानो से डटकर जिया
वो जिंदगी सफल कर जायेगा
वरना खाली हाथ आया था
खाली हाथ ही जायेगा ।

Destinations are not claimed by mere wishing,
they are seized through struggle and sweat.
Wings are torn, reshaped, and earned
not gifted to those who only dream of flight.
Whoever stands unbroken before the storm
will carve success out of life itself.
The rest arrive empty handed,
and leave the same way
with nothing but regret.

47. आएगी कई मुश्किलें तेरी राहो मे

आएगी कई मुश्किलें तेरी राहो मे
उनसे सामना करने की तू हिम्मत तो रख
दिल मे प्यार और चेहरे पर हसी
ऐसे ही खुद पर विश्वास रख
तू पा लेगा जो भी तुझे चाहिए
बस तू अपनी दौड़ जारी रख ।

Many challenges will rise along your path,
just hold the courage to face them when they appear.
Carry love quietly in your heart,
a steady smile upon your face,
and keep faith in who you are.
You will reach all that you seek
just keep moving forward,
and let your journey continue without pause.

I CAN
I WILL
I MUST
PLAN
1.
2.
3.
4.
Don't think that life will pass just somehow, my friend.
Believe in yourself. You are stronger than you think.

48. कट जाये जैसे तैसे ये जिंदगी

कट जाये जैसे तैसे ये जिंदगी
ऐ दोस्त ऐसी सोच ना तू रख
है तुझमे भी काबिलियत
तू जरा खुद को तो परख
माना के होंगे तुझमे भी ऐब खूब सारे
पर यु मायूस होकर खुदको कमज़ोर ना कर
तेरी लगन ही है तेरी ताकत
तू बस खुद से वफादारी जारी रख ।

Don't settle for merely getting through this life, my friend,
don't let such small thoughts take root.
You carry ability within you too
pause, and give yourself the chance to see it.
Yes, you may have your share of flaws, we all do, many of us.
But don't let disappointment turn you against yourself.
Your dedication is your true strength.
Just stay loyal to your effort,
and keep faith with who you are.

49. एहसान उसका भी तो चुकाना होगा

जी ली जिंदगी जितनी जीनी थी खुद के लिये
थोड़ा अब अपने देश का भी खयाल रख
एहसान उसका भी तो चुकाना होगा तुझे
तू तरक्की कर बस तिरंगा याद रख।

You've lived enough of life for yourself,
now spare a thought for your country too.
This nation has given you more than you know
now is the time to give back through your progress.
Move ahead, succeed,
just keep the tricolor remembered in every stride.

A CHANCE IN YOUR HANDS
OPPORTUNITY
FAILURE?
TRY
TOGETHER WE CAN ACHIEVE MORE

50. अपनो से दोस्ती बनाये रख

हाथ मे मौका है तो निकल पड़ पथ पर
तू यू ही हार की फिकर ना कर
ऐसे दौर में अपने ही तो आते है काम
तू बस अपनो से दोस्ती बनाये रख ।

When opportunity rises into your hands,
do not pause, march forward and take the path that calls you.
Let fear fall behind like dust in your wake,
you were never meant to kneel before defeat.
In times that test your soul,
it is your own people who stand shoulder to shoulder,
unshaken, unbroken, beside you.
Hold those bonds like a banner held high,
this unity that will lead you through every storm
and lifts you toward victory.

PLATFORM
7
DON'T STOP
UNTIL
YOU'RE
PROUD
ONE DAY
ALL THIS
HARD WORK
WILL PAY OFF
DEEP WORK
MINDSET
Atomic Habits
STAY
HUNGRY
STAY
FOOLISH
FOCUS
DEDICATION
PATIENCE
FAILURE
FAILURE
REJECTION
DISCIPLINE
HARD WORK

51. जिनको लगन हो अपने ध्येय से

मैंने अपनी ख्वाईशो को हमेशा आसमान से ऊपर रखा है,
ज़िंदगी की भागदौड़ चाहे 'बसों और ट्रेनों' में गुज़री हो,
पर सपने तो बस 'Rolls-Royce' ही दिखाती रही है ॥
रुख़ बदलेगी हवा इक दिन और झुकेगी ये दुनिया मेरे आगे,
मैं मानता हूँ कोई यूही एक दिन में बड़ा आदमी नहीं बनता,
जिनको लगन हो अपने ध्येय से उनकी तो कामयाबी भी राह तकती है ॥

I have always set my desires higher than the sky.
Though life's rush may have carried me
through buses and trains,
my dreams have only ever ridden in a RollsRoyce.
One day the wind will change its course,
and the world will bow before me.
I know no one becomes great in a single day,
but those devoted to their purpose
find that success itself waits for them along the path.

I'll always be with you..
HER WAY
MY WAY
FRIENDSHIP IS GOD

52. इश्क में मसरुफ़ इतना थे हम

इश्क में मसरूफ़ इतना थे हम
की दुनिया हमसे आगे निकल गई
हर मुकाम पे साथ दूंगी बोलने वाली
इक मोड़ आया तो अपने रास्ते निकल गई
दोस्तो ने दिया सहारा जब भी जरूरत थी
प्यार को खुदा मान बैठे, दोस्ती खुदा निकल गयी
बेइंतहा चाहा था जिसे उसने तो पहचान भी ना दिखाई
जब गली से उसके मेरी अर्थी निकल गई ।

I was so lost in love that the world quietly moved ahead without me.
The one who promised to stand by me at every step, took a different road when the first turn came.
Friends became my support whenever I truly needed it.
I gave love a respect as god, only to realize, it was friendship that was divine.
I loved her beyond measure, but she never claimed my name.
And when my final journey crossed her street, she watched as though I were a stranger she had never known.

53. पैसे कमाने निकले थे सुबह

पैसे कमाने निकले थे सुबह घर से दूर
काम में इतना उलझ गए की
पता ही नही चला कब शाम निकल गई
दूसरो को खुश रखने में अपनी जान लूटा दी
जब खुदकी बारी आई तो जवानी निकल गई ।

I left home at dawn, chasing a living far away,
so caught in the weight of work
that I never noticed
when evening quietly slipped past me.
I spent my life pouring myself out
to keep others smiling, standing, whole.
And when it was finally my turn to live,
my youth had already faded into memory.

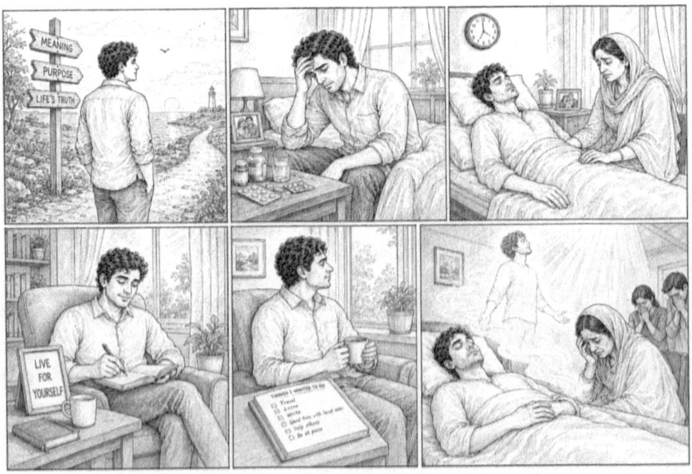
MEANING
PURPOSE
LIFE'S TRUTH
LIVE FOR YOURSELF

54. जिंदगी गुमनाम थी और गुमनाम ही रही

अब जब जिंदगी का सार पता चला,
तो तबियत ने हमसे मुंह मोड़ लिया,
जिंदगी गुमनाम थी और गुमनाम ही रही,
सोचा था अब जियेंगे कुछ दिन खुद के लिए,
और यहां शरीर से आत्मा निकल गई ।

Just when I began to understand the meaning of life,
my body quietly turned its face away from me.
Life passed in anonymity and remained so till the end.
I had thought at last
I would live a few moments for myself,
but before those moments could begin,
the soul loosened its grip
and gently slipped away from the body.

MARKET
STATION
HOSPITAL
TEMPLE
DEATH
EVEN YOU
LOOK BEAUTIFUL
NOW

55. मुझे मौत भी हसीन लगती है

हम तो ख़ुशमिज़ाज थे तेरे आने से पहले
अब तो हम होश में भी कम ही रहते है
तुम तो छोड़ गए हमे बीच चौराहें
हम हर राहगुज़र से तुम्हारा पता पूछते है
यू तो ज़िंदगी इस क़दर बरबाद कर गई हो तुम
के अब तो मुझे मौत भी हसीन लगती है ।

I was a cheerful soul before you came into my life,
now I barely remain myself even in my waking hours.
You left me standing alone at life's crossroads,
while I keep searching for you in every passing face.
You walked away, but took my peace with you.
My days are ruined by the memories you left behind.
You have broken my life so completely,
that even death now seems more beautiful than living without you.

www.ingramcontent.com/pod-product-compliance
Lightning Source LLC
LaVergne TN
LVHW090417210926
848480LV00002B/601